Mom, tell me abo Diwali

AMY SINGH'S BOOKS:

Diwali is one of India's biggest and most important festivals.

The festival is celebrated in the Hindu month of Kartika during October or November.

It is a festival of lights.
Diwali means rows of lighted lamps.

During the festival, we worship Goddess Lakshmi for wisdom and wealth.

We also worship Lord Ganesha for prosperity and good welfare.

Diwali is celebrated for five days.

It as a perfect occasion to strengthen family and relationships, and everybody celebrates it with joy.

Day 1 is Dhanteras. We clean our houses.

We also do some shopping, particularly for gold or silver articles.

Day 2 is Narak Chaturdasi. We decorate our homes.

We decorate entrances with Rangoli.

Women decorate their hands with henna designs.

Families prepare homemade sweets for the main celebration.

Day 3 is Lakshmi Puja. People wear new or their best clothes and go for puja.

We make diyas lit. Pujas are offered to Lakshmi.

In the evening, people open their doors and windows to welcome Lakshmi.

After the puja, people go outside and celebrate by lighting up fireworks (patakhe).

Day 4 is Padwa. This day we celebrate the love between wife and husband.

It is also the beginning of new year. We visit our family and friends with gifts and wishes.

Day 5 is Bhai dooj. We celebrate sister-brother loving relationship. Brothers travel to meet their sisters and sisters prepare a meal for them.

Happy Diwali!

Do you like this book?
We will appreciate your review on Amazon.
Thank you.

Printed in Great Britain
by Amazon